EDGE BOOKS™

NASCAR RACING

Under the Hood

by Matt Doeden

Consultant:
Suzanne Wise, Librarian
Stock Car Racing Collection, Belk Library
Appalachian State University
Boone, North Carolina

Capstone press®
Mankato, Minnesota

Edge Books are published by Capstone Press,
151 Good Counsel Drive, P.O. Box 669, Mankato, Minnesota 56002.
www.capstonepress.com

Library of Congress Cataloging-in-Publication Data
Doeden, Matt.
    Under the hood / by Matt Doeden.
      p. cm.—(Edge books. NASCAR racing)
    Summary: "Describes how a modern NASCAR stock car is built, including the
engine, body, and special safety features"—Provided by publisher.
    Includes bibliographical references and index.
    ISBN–13: 978-1-4296-0085-9 (hardcover)
    ISBN–10: 1-4296-0085-3 (hardcover)
    1. Stock cars (Automobiles)—Design and construction—Juvenile literature.
2. Stock car racing—United States—Juvenile literature. I. Title.
TL236.28.D65 2008
629.228—dc22   2007000251

Editorial Credits

Aaron Sautter, editor; Jason Knudson, set designer; Patrick D. Dentinger, book designer;
    Jo Miller, photo researcher

Photo Credits

AP/Wide World Photos/Chris Gardner, 11; Chris O'Meara, 25; Jim Cole, 5;
    Mike Silverwood, 24
Corbis/GT Images/George Tiedemann, 6, 20–21; Icon SMI/Craig Peterson, 27;
    NewSport/George Tiedemann, 14, 17–18, 28
Getty Images Inc./Jamie Squire, 9; for NASCAR/Streeter Lecka, 10
The Sharpe Image/Sam Sharpe, cover, 12, 15, 23

1 2 3 4 5 6 12 11 10 09 08 07

Table of Contents

Chapter 1
Small Adjustment, Big Results 4

Chapter 2
Building the Car 8

Chapter 3
Power to Move 16

Chapter 4
Safety Behind the Wheel 22

Stock Car Diagram 20

Nextel Cup Car Specifications 29

Glossary 30

Read More 31

Internet Sites 31

Index 32

Small Adjustment, Big Results

Dale Earnhardt Jr. didn't think he had much chance to win the 2000 Pontiac Excitement 400. It was only the second race of his career, and his car was handling poorly. He was falling farther and farther back in the pack.

On his radio, Earnhardt described what was wrong to his crew chief, Tony Eury. The rear tires weren't gripping the track surface very well. The car's back end felt like it was sliding around through every turn. Earnhardt thought the car's suspension was loose.

Eury told the pit crew what was wrong. The team knew how to fix the problem. The next time Earnhardt brought the car down pit road, they were ready. One pit crew member stuck a wrench under the back of the car to adjust the springs. The car's chassis dipped a fraction of an inch closer to the track.

Stock cars with loose suspensions are often hard to control in the turns.

Learn about:

➜ **Problems on the track**

➜ **An important pit stop**

➜ **Winning the race**

Dale Earnhardt Jr. likes to do burnouts after a big win.

It seemed like a small change, but Earnhardt noticed the difference right away. Suddenly, he was passing cars. Soon Earnhardt trailed only his famous father, Dale Earnhardt Sr., for the lead. With his car working so well, Junior easily passed his father. On the final lap, he held off a charging Terry Labonte to earn his second career victory.

In victory lane, Junior celebrated with Eury and the pit crew. He reminded TV viewers that good driving wasn't enough to win a race. By making a small adjustment, his team turned a poorly handling car into the fastest car on the track.

"Right there at the end, Tony [Eury] and the guys got the car where it was giving me all it could give me. And I drove it as hard as I could drive."

—Dale Earnhardt Jr., from *Little E's Big Win* by David Poole, Triumph Books, 2004.

CHAPTER 2

Building the Car

Thrilling passes, wild wrecks, and pure speed make NASCAR exciting. But what goes into a winning car? Stock cars have hundreds of parts. If even one part doesn't work correctly, it could mean the difference between victory lane and last place.

The Frame and Body

Every race car must fit within NASCAR's rules. When a new car is built, the team needs to follow specific guidelines.

Race teams begin building their cars with a strong frame, or chassis. The chassis acts as a stock car's skeleton. Strong steel tubes give the car its basic shape and help hold it together.

A tool called a jig holds the tubes in place while the builders weld them together. Builders use the jig to make sure the chassis fits NASCAR's strict standards.

Race teams build strong frames to keep stock cars stable and safe.

Learn about:

→ Following NASCAR rules

→ Tuning the suspension

→ Keeping cool

The car's body fits over the frame. Fabricators shape panels of sheet metal to create the body. Like the chassis, the body must be shaped correctly to follow NASCAR's standards. If a car's shape doesn't fit the guidelines, it won't be allowed to race.

The race team attaches the car's body to the frame.

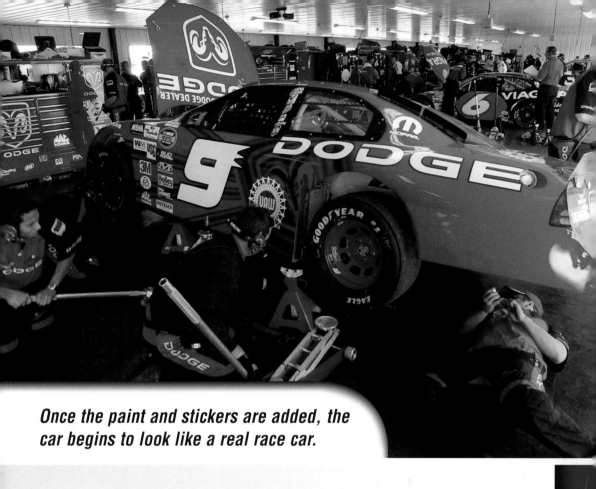

Once the paint and stickers are added, the car begins to look like a real race car.

Once the body is shaped and attached, teams grind the metal until it's perfectly smooth. Teams then paint and detail the car with numbers, decals, and sponsor logos. The car finally begins to look like what fans see on the track.

Suspension Systems

Once the body is ready, teams work on the suspension system. This system of springs and shock absorbers connects the body to the car's wheels and axles. Suspensions affect how cars handle on the track. Tight suspensions make cars hard to turn. Suspensions that are too loose make cars hard to control.

shock absorber

spring

Springs and shock absorbers play an important part in how a car handles on the track.

Pit crews often make small adjustments to a car's suspension during a race. One adjustment involves the amount of weight each spring holds. This is called adjusting the wedge. If a car's weight isn't balanced correctly, it won't run smoothly. The tires can also wear out faster on one side.

Pit crews can also add or remove spring rubbers. These small rubber pieces fit between the coils of the car's springs. Adding a spring rubber helps make the suspension firmer. Removing one loosens it up.

"I love driving these cars . . . my pit crew was awesome all night—every stop was great, and we gained each time we made a stop."
—Dale Earnhardt Jr., Motorsport.com, 8/26/2006

Crews change tires as fast as possible during pit stops.

Tires and Brakes

Radial tires called slicks fit over the car's wheels. NASCAR tires are made to handle extreme heat from friction with the track. Slicks don't have treads like street tires. Instead, they are smooth to get a better grip on the track.

NASCAR teams fill tires with a gas called nitrogen. Nitrogen contains less moisture than regular air. As tires heat up, water vapor trapped inside expands. Keeping down the moisture level makes tires more stable and reduces blowouts.

Large disc brakes fit inside the wheels. During races, cars often need to slow down quickly. Some drivers wait until the last possible second to slow down. This increases friction between the brakes and the wheels.

On short tracks that require lots of braking, the brakes can get so hot they glow red. To avoid brake failure, teams add vents that force air over the brakes. The air cools the brakes and keeps them from wearing down too quickly.

Brakes need to be strong to handle the intense braking during a race.

CHAPTER 3

Power to Move

Stock cars need fast acceleration and a high top speed to win. Without a good engine under the hood, a driver has no chance for victory.

Horsepower

Stock car engines are all about horsepower. Stock cars have powerful V8 engines. Eight cylinders arranged in a "V" shape burn fuel for lots of power. Engines in most regular cars produce about 200 horsepower. But stock car engines produce 750 horsepower or more. All this power lets stock cars scream down the track at up to 200 miles (320 kilometers) per hour. This is the power racing teams need to win.

Powerful V8 engines are tuned perfectly for every race.

Learn about:

→ Engine power
→ Shifting gears
→ Gear setups

With powerful engines and well-tuned transmissions, stock cars can tear up the track at amazing speeds.

Transmissions

A car's engine sends power to the wheels through the transmission. Stock cars have manual transmissions. Several gears inside the transmission let drivers control the car's speed. Drivers use a pedal called a clutch and a gearshift to change gears. Drivers start in first gear. As the car gains speed, they upshift to higher gears. When they want to slow down, drivers downshift to lower gears.

Teams set up transmissions specifically for each race. The gear setup determines the top speed for each gear. When the gears are widely spaced, the car has a high top speed but slow acceleration. If the gears are narrowly spaced, the car speeds up faster, but its top speed is lower. Teams have to find just the right balance to build a winning car.

STOCK CAR DIAGRAM
*Chevrolet Monte Carlo

1. **Roof flaps**
2. **Slicks**
3. **Safety net**
4. **Roll cage**
5. **Windshield**
6. **Jack point**
7. **Spoiler**
8. **Sponsor stickers**

Safety Behind the Wheel

High speeds and aggressive driving make NASCAR a dangerous sport. Drivers trust their cars with their lives. Race teams build safety features into a car to keep drivers safe.

Chassis Safety

Many safety features are built into the chassis and body of a stock car. The roll cage is one of the most important. The frame's strongest and thickest tubes form a cage that surrounds the driver. Roll cages can withstand strong impacts. Even during flips and rollovers, the roll cage prevents the car's body from crushing the driver.

Strong roll cages surround drivers to keep them safe in a crash.

Learn about:

→ Roll cages
→ The HANS device
→ NASCAR specifications

Roof flaps are another important safety feature. These flaps open only if air is forced over a car that is traveling backward. Sometimes when a stock car spins out of control, it ends up going backward at a high speed. The car then tends to fly into the air. The roof flaps push down on the car to help keep all four tires on the ground.

Roof flaps pop up when a car travels backward at high speed.

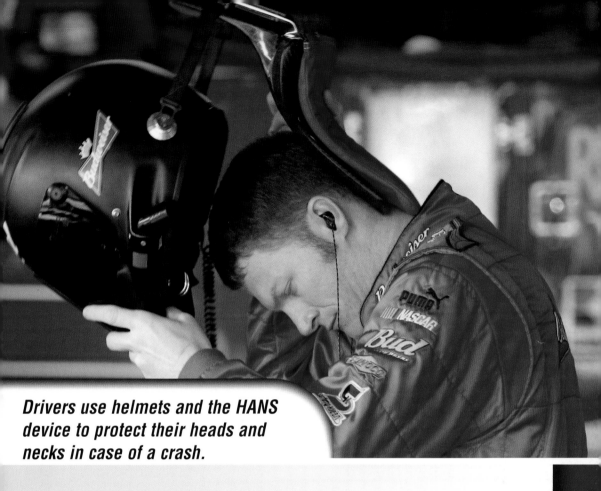

Drivers use helmets and the HANS device to protect their heads and necks in case of a crash.

Teams add many more safety features to cars. Special seats and restraints hold the driver's body and head firmly in place. The Head And Neck Safety (HANS) device keeps a driver's head from snapping forward or sideways in a bad wreck. Window nets keep drivers' arms from flying out of the window in a crash. Windshields are made from a strong material called Lexan that is almost impossible to break.

Engine Safety

Other safety features protect drivers in case of engine trouble. Firewalls separate the engine from the car's cockpit. The walls protect drivers if the engine catches on fire. Drivers can also use a kill switch on the steering wheel to instantly turn off the engine in an emergency.

On the largest tracks, the turns are so wide that drivers don't even touch the brakes. This can lead to unsafe speeds. To slow cars down, NASCAR requires teams to add small metal plates inside the car's engine. These restrictor plates reduce the flow of air to the engine. With less air, the engine can't burn fuel as quickly. The car's horsepower is reduced, slowing it down through the turns.

"I feel a lot safer today than I did five years ago. Every new improvement that comes along to make us even safer certainly helps. You can never be too safe when you're a race car driver."

—Joe Nemecheck, from *Striving for Safety* by Jerry Bonkowski, Yahoo! Sports, 2/17/2006.

But restrictor plates don't always have the effect NASCAR officials want. Though the cars travel at a slower speed, they tend to group together in large packs. If just one driver loses control, many cars can be involved in a wreck. Drivers often talk about avoiding "the big one" at Daytona and Talledega.

Restrictor plates slow down cars, but they're often blamed for big wrecks on NASCAR's largest tracks.

Burnouts are a popular way to show off the power of a winning stock car.

Winning Big

There's a lot going on under a stock car's hood. Winning teams need more than a good driver. The car needs to have a strong frame and body, a well-tuned suspension system, and a powerful engine. Big wins may end at the finish line, but they always start with a well-built car.

Nextel Cup Car Specifications

Length:	202.5 inches (514 centimeters)
Width:	74 inches (188 centimeters)
Height:	51 inches (130 centimeters)
Weight:	3,400 pounds (1,540 kilograms)
Tires:	28 x 12 x 15 inches
	(71 x 30 x 38 centimeters)
Engine type:	V8
Engine size:	358 cubic inches
	(5,867 cubic centimeters)
Horsepower:	750 hp
Top Speed:	210 miles (340 kilometers) per hour
Suspension:	Independent
Drive:	Rear-wheel drive
Brakes:	4-wheel disc brakes
Transmission:	4-speed manual
Acceleration:	0–60 mph (0–100 kph)
	in about 3.5 seconds

Glossary

chassis (CHASS-ee)—the frame on which the body of a vehicle is built

clutch (KLUHCH)—a pedal that a driver presses to change gears in a car with a manual transmission

fabricator (FAB-ri-kate-uhr)—a team member who builds and shapes the body of a stock car

horsepower (HORSS-pow-ur)—a unit for measuring an engine's power

jack point (JAK POYNT)—a small piece of metal welded to the chassis to assist in jacking up the car

restrictor plate (ri-STRIKT-ur PLAYT)—a device that limits the power of a race car's engine; the restrictor plate keeps down the car's speed for safety

slick (SLIK)—a racing tire made with a smooth, soft surface to get maximum grip on the track

suspension system (suh-SPEN-shuhn SISS-tuhm)—a system of springs and shock absorbers connecting the main body of a car to the wheels and axles

transmission (transs-MISH-uhn)—the series of gears that send power from the engine to the wheels

Read More

Buckley, James Jr. *NASCAR.* DK Eyewitness Books. New York: DK, 2005.

DeBoard, Will. *Building a Stock Car: The Need for More Speed.* The World of NASCAR. Excelsior, Minn.: Tradition Books, 2002.

Doeden, Matt. *NASCAR's Wildest Wrecks.* NASCAR Racing. Mankato, Minn.: Capstone Press, 2005.

Internet Sites

FactHound offers a safe, fun way to find Internet sites related to this book. All of the sites on FactHound have been researched by our staff.

Here's how:
1. Visit *www.facthound.com*
2. Choose your grade level.
3. Type in this book ID code **1429600853** for age-appropriate sites. You may also browse subjects by clicking on letters, or by clicking on pictures and words.
4. Click on the **Fetch It** button.

FactHound will fetch the best sites for you!

Index

acceleration, 16, 19
adjustments, 7, 13
axles, 12

bodies, 10, 11, 12, 22, 28
brakes, 15, 26

chassis, 4, 8, 9, 10, 22, 28
clutch, 19

Earnhardt Jr., Dale, 4, 6, 7, 13
Earnhardt Sr., Dale, 7
engines, 16, 17, 18, 19, 26, 28
Eury, Tony, 4, 7

friction, 14, 15

gearshift, 19
guidelines, 8, 10, 29

HANS device, 25
helmets, 25
horsepower, 16, 26

jigs, 8

Labonte, Terry, 7
Lexan, 25

Nemecheck, Joe, 26

pit crews, 4, 7, 13, 14
Pontiac Excitement 400, 4

restrictor plates, 26–27
roll cages, 21, 22, 23
roof flaps, 21, 24

safety features, 9, 22–27
shape, 8, 10, 11
shock absorbers, 12
speed, 16, 18, 19, 22, 24, 26, 27
spoiler, 21
sponsor logos, 11, 21
springs, 4, 12, 13
spring rubbers, 13
suspension systems, 4, 5, 12–13, 28

teams, 4, 7, 8, 9, 10, 11, 12, 15, 16, 19, 22, 25, 28
tires, 4, 13, 14, 21, 24
transmissions, 18, 19

wheels, 12, 14, 15, 19
window nets, 21, 25
windshields, 21, 25
wrecks, 8, 25, 27